Published by Creative Education
123 South Broad Street, Mankato, Minnesota 56001
Creative Education is an imprint of The Creative Company

Designed by Stephanie Blumenthal
Production Design by Melinda Belter

Photographs by Cindy Kilgore Brown, Martin Honig, Barrett & MacKay, C. Allan
Morgan, Dusty Perin, Leonard Lee Rue III, Len Rue, Jr., & Kevin Schafer

Copyright © 2000 Creative Education.
International copyrights reserved in all countries.
No part of this book may be reproduced in any form without
written permission from the publisher.

Library of Congress Cataloging-in-Publication Data

Allen, Deborah, 1954–
Puffins / by Deborah Allen
p. cm. — (Let's Investigate)
Includes glossary and index
Summary: Describes the physical characteristics and habits of these
coastal marine birds, as well as threats to their survival.
ISBN 0-88682-610-1
1. Puffins—Juvenile literature. [1. Puffins.] I. Title. II. Series.
III. Series: Let's Investigate (Mankato, Minn.)
QL696.C42A58   1999
598.3'3—dc21   98-17172

First edition

2 4 6 8 9 7 5 3 1

PUFFINS

DEBORAH ALLEN

Creative Education

PUFFIN

Sea travelers who first encountered puffins called them "sea parrots."

Birds are feathered animals; many can fly, but no other bird looks or acts quite like a puffin. Silly and serious, puffins are sometimes called "the **penguins** of the north." Like penguins, puffins walk upright and use their wings to swim underwater. Unlike penguins, however, puffins can also fly.

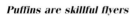

Puffins are skillful flyers

PUFFIN

FACT

The Atlantic puffin is the national emblem of Iceland.

Above, a puffin colony
Right, puffins have colorful bills

KINDS OF PUFFINS

Puffins belong to the large family of seabirds called *Alcidae*, commonly known auks. Cold-weather birds, puffins spend most of their time at sea, floating on waves and diving to catch small fish.

There are three species of puffins: the Atlantic puffin, the horned puffin, and the tufted puffin, as well as a close relative called the rhinoceros auklet.

The Atlantic puffin wears a tuxedo of black and white feathers. Its bill, almost as big as its head, is red, yellow, blue, and off-white. Bright, black eyes give the puffin a sly look, as though it were planning to play a trick on someone.

PUFFIN

FACT

In Vestmannaeyjar, young puffins sometimes get lost on their way to sea; people often catch them and put them in the water.

Below, Atlantic puffling

PUFFIN

Shearwaters, birds named for their behavior of skimming the water's surface in search of fish, may nest just inside a puffin's burrow.

The horned puffin looks very much like the Atlantic puffin, except that its bill is yellow and red. In summer, the horned puffin grows a small black "horn" of hard skin above each eye.

Horned puffin

icknamed "old man of the sea" in Alaska, the tufted puffin is black with white cheeks. Long, straw-colored tufts sweep back from its face like overgrown eyebrows. Its bill is orange-red and olive green.

PUFFIN
FASHION

Native Americans in the Aleutian Islands once wore heavy coats, or parkas, made from the skin of puffins.

**Above, bald eagle
Left, tufted puffin**

PUFFIN
SPEED

Adult puffins can fly at speeds of up to 50 miles (80.5 km) per hour.

Right, rhinoceros auklet
Opposite, Atlantic puffin nesting colony

The rhinoceros auklet looks very different from the true puffins. Its bill is not as big or as brightly colored, and it has a large ridge called a horn at the base. The rhinoceros auklet has pale, wispy plumes of feathers on its head.

PUFFIN
HUNTER

On the island of St. Kilda, in the Hebrides west of Scotland, people once hunted puffins using a long stick with a noose at the end.

Top right, this puffin is taking flight
Bottom right, this puffin is landing

PUFFIN BODIES

The rhinoceros auklet, the largest of the puffin varieties, is no more than 16 inches (40.6 cm) from bill to tail. The smallest is the Atlantic puffin, at 10 to 12 inches (24 to 30 cm) in length.

Short wings and powerful breast muscles make it easy for puffins to swim underwater. Floating on the surface, puffins uses their webbed feet to paddle like a duck.

Puffins are accurate flyers; they can zoom straight into their burrows without stopping to land.

A puffin's bill is colorful only during the nesting season, while puffins mate. In the fall, pieces of the bill flake off, leaving the puffin with the small, drab bill that it will wear in winter. Puffins are the only auks to shed their bills, but not the only bird to go through such changes. White pelicans, for example, grow a knob on top of their bills and shed it after the eggs are laid.

Tufted puffins

PUFFIN
FACT

Puffins can't turn quickly in flight, which makes it easy for people to catch flying puffins in nets.

Atlantic puffin preening its feathers

The bill is a powerful tool. It can crack open shellfish and crustaceans and can hold more than 60 fish at one time. The roof of the puffin's mouth has small backward-pointing spines that keep food in place as it is being carried.

Puffins are **warm-blooded** animals that spend most of their time in cold water. To stay warm, a puffin "waterproofs" its feathers. When it **preens,** the puffin spreads a thin coating of oil over its feathers. This oil is produced in a **gland** at the base of the puffin's tail.

Unlike most animals, puffins can drink salt water. Too much salt in an animal's (or human's) body can cause it to **dehydrate,** but the puffin's kidneys are designed to remove much of the salt from its bloodstream. Glands in the puffin's nostrils also help remove salt from the body.

Interestingly, many species of reptiles are equipped with similar glands that remove excess salt from their bodies as well.

PUFFIN
PLUNGE

Puffins can hold their breath longer than a minute while diving to depths of 200 feet (61 m).

15

Horned puffin making an aggressive gesture called "yawning"

PUFFIN

FABLE

An old story tells of a "Puffin King" who instructs the other puffins of his colony when to return for nesting in the spring.

Right, puffins on Machias Seal Island in the state of Maine

PUFFIN POPULATIONS

Puffins live in **colonies** in North America. The Atlantic puffin nests along the northern coasts of the Atlantic Ocean, from the British Isles and Maine over to Greenland and Iceland. The other puffins nest in areas of the northern Pacific Ocean, as far north as the Bering Sea. The rhinoceros auklet prefers cold regions, but it has been known to nest as far south as California and Japan.

There are 15 to 20 million Atlantic puffins in the world, five million in the Westmann Islands, or Vestmannaeyjar, of Iceland. Roughly 5,000 people live in Vestmannaeyjar, so puffins there outnumber people by 1,000 to 1. The largest of the Westmann Islands is only 4.7 miles (7.5 km) long. Nearly 4 million tufted puffins, 1.5 million horned puffins, and 1 million rhinoceros auklets live in the north Pacific.

PUFFIN
F A C T

Studies show that puffin growth and development is connected to the number of daylight hours.

Below, a sign in Newfoundland

TOWN OF WITLESS BAY
· INCORPORATED 1986 ·
HOME OF THE NORTH ATLANTIC PUFFIN
WELCOME

PUFFIN

An early species of auk, the family to which puffins belong, first appeared 70 million years ago.

18

REPRODUCTION AND GROWTH

In spring, puffins gather in a large flock near the island or section of coastline where they will nest. Like other birds that nest in colonies, puffins return to the same area each year. A courting male puffin will shake his head to tell the female puffin to join him. Male and female puffins often rub their bills together. This is called "billing." After the male and female bill, they may mate. Mating takes place on the water.

A puffin pair billing

When the pair is ready to build a nest, the male puffin, with help from the female, digs a burrow in the soil at the top of a cliff. The Atlantic puffin's burrow is two to four feet (61 to 122 cm) long. The burrow of the rhinoceros auklet is a tunnel up to 10 feet (3 m) long. Some puffins simply nest in the crevices between rocks.

PUFFIN
F A C T

A puffin doesn't chew—the food is swallowed whole while still alive.

19

Horned puffin pair at nest hole

PUFFIN

When in the water, a frightened puffin will dive to escape from danger instead of flying away.

Above, black-backed gull
Right, Atlantic puffin
gathering nest material

Each pair of puffins has its own **terri-tory,** but puffins often visit their neighbors. A puffin may even go into another puffin's bur-row, especially when there's no one home.

Puffins nest once in a season and lay only one egg. They may put dried grass or feathers in the burrow, but the female may also lay her egg on the burrow's bare floor. The egg is about the size of a chicken egg and is white or off-white, sometimes with faint blotches or scrawls.

A puffin has two **brood patches,** one on each side of its body. After the female lays the egg, the male and the female take turns **incubating** it. In six to seven weeks the egg will hatch and a puffin chick will emerge. The new chick has no feathers yet; rather, it is covered with **down.**

PUFFIN
SHADOW

Rhinoceros auklets enter and leave their burrows only during the dark.

21

Snowy owls prey on young puffins

PUFFIN
NAME

The word "puffin" was first used by observers to describe the fat, puffy puffin chicks.

Above, razorbills with a group of puffins
Right, Atlantic puffling

The puffin parents care for their chick, or puffling, for another six to seven weeks. During this time, they feed the chick, whose down is gradually replaced by smooth, new **plumage.** When it is ready to leave the burrow, the young puffin heads out to sea to find fish on its own, though its bill is still much smaller than an adult's.

Young puffins will remain with the colony. They may flirt with other puffins or practice digging a burrow, but they usually won't make their own nests until they are five years old.

PUFFIN
ANGER

Opening their bill is a behavior that puffins exhibit to express their anger.

PUFFIN
MYSTERY

Atlantic puffins live 25 years, but scientists still don't know how long tufted puffins, horned puffins, and rhinoceros auklets live.

Horned puffins

PUFFIN
PARENT

If another species of bird lays an egg in a puffin burrow, the puffin will care for it.

PUFFIN
ITCH

Puffins sometimes get fleas in their feathers; these tiny insects suck the puffins' blood and make them feel itchy.

24

Right, puffins are very curious birds
Opposite, Atlantic puffin with herring

A puffin's life isn't always easy. A warm ocean current may cause fish to swim far below the surface, where the puffin can't catch them, or storms at sea may make it impossible to hunt.

Sometimes as a puffin comes back to its burrow with fish in its mouth, a herring gull may try to steal them. Other birds that steal fish from puffins are the lesser black-backed gulls and black-tailed gulls.

PUFFIN
BONES

Birds have hollow bones that make their bodies lightweight, but the wing bones of puffins are solid to help them stay underwater.

Peregrine falcons (above) and grey seals (below) eat puffins

The larger great black-backed gulls often kill and eat puffins, sometimes surprising a puffin by waiting outside its burrow. **Instinct** tells puffins to be careful when they travel from land to sea and back again, especially if gulls are present in the area. Puffins can also become meals for great skuas, ravens, bald eagles, snowy owls, and peregrine falcons. The water usually offers safety, but sometimes puffins are snatched by seals. A puffin was once even found inside the stomach of an anglerfish!

Seagulls rarely attack adult puffins

PUFFINS AND HUMANS

In the early days of human settlement in America, it was common for ships to stop at seabird colonies to gather eggs and to capture birds for food. By 1900, many seabird colonies had been wiped out by human interference. In addition, animals not native to puffin **habitats** were introduced to the new lands by humans traveling there. Many of these animals, such as minks, Norway rats, Arctic foxes, and house cats, kill and eat puffins.

PUFFIN
BLUNDER

Puffin colonies sometimes dig so many burrows on an island that the ground caves in, forcing the puffins to find a new home.

PUFFIN
PLAN

Rhinoceros auklets are smart birds; they sometimes herd fish into groups by blowing air bubbles all around them.

A puffin hunter in the Westmann Islands, Iceland

Atlantic puffins are still hunted in Iceland and the Faroe Islands. In Vestmannaeyjar 60,000 to 100,000 puffins are caught with nets each summer. Puffin breast meat is often smoked and then eaten cold. The meat is dark and oily, with a slightly fishy flavor. Puffin meat is even sold in some Iceland supermarkets.

ommercial fishing has also affected the **ecosystem** in which puffins try to survive. Fishermen take much of the puffins' food supply, leaving puffin colonies with little to eat. In addition, each year thousands of puffins get caught in fishing nets and drown. Accidents such as oil and chemical spills endanger puffins as well.

PUFFIN
TREK

Instinct tells a young puffin that it's safer to leave the burrow and head to sea at night while hungry gulls are asleep.

Below, Atlantic puffin

PUFFIN
STATUES

In Iceland and the Faroe Islands puffins are stuffed with saw-dust and sold to tourists as souvenirs.

PUFFIN
COLORS

The bright colors on the puffin's bill fade slowly throughout the nesting season; also, the puffin's orange-red legs become flesh-colored.

Right, horned puffin Far right, puffins are tagged and followed by ornithologists

CONSERVATION

In Maine, a program called The Puffin Project worked to reestablish a small puffin colony on Eastern Egg Rock, where puffins had once nested before human interference. Puffin chicks were taken from Newfoundland and raised on the island in artificial burrows. Eventually some of these chicks returned to Eastern Egg Rock to nest.

The Migratory Bird Treaty Act in the United States and the Wild Birds Protection Act in England both protect puffins and many other wild birds.

Puffins have been the subject of many studies by bird scientists, or ornithologists, but there is still much that isn't known about them. If humans work to preserve the ocean by limiting pollution and overfishing, our planet will remain a healthy habitat for many of our world's animals, including the silly and serious "penguins of the north."

Glossary

Brood patches are the areas of bare skin on a bird's breast that allow body heat to escape; the bird rests this skin over its eggs while **incubating** them, or keeping them warm so they will hatch.

Colonies are groups of animals, such as birds, that nest together in one place.

Human and animal bodies need water to survive; when a body does not have enough water, it will **dehydrate,** leading to the victim's death.

The soft, fluffy feathers on a bird is called **down.**

An **ecosystem** is a group of plants and animals living together. Ecosystems can be large, like the whole world, or very small, like a pond or forest.

A **gland** is an organ that produces certain substances inside the body of a human or an animal; bodies contain many different kinds of glands.

Habitats are the environments where plants or animals naturally live and grow.

Instinct is a natural impulse that causes humans and animals to respond to certain things in their environment; for example, it is a natural instinct to want food or to be fearful of danger.

Penguins are aquatic birds with short legs and sleek feathers; they swim, but do not fly, and live only in the southern hemisphere, where they eat fish.

A covering of feathers is called **plumage.**

When a bird **preens** it cleans and repairs its feathers.

A **territory** is the area where an animal lives; it defends this area from invasion by other animals of its kind.

A **warm-blooded** animal has a normally constant and warm body temperature regardless of the temperature of its environment. It needs fur or feathers to keep warm.

Index